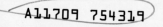

Ring Out, Wild Bells

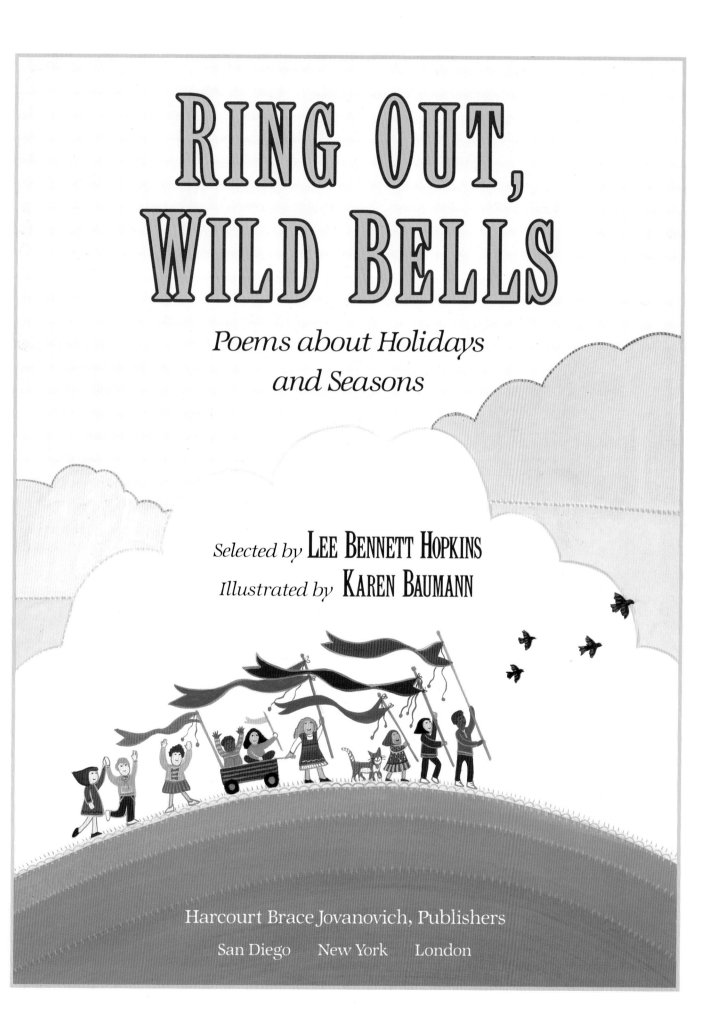

RING OUT, WILD BELLS

Poems about Holidays and Seasons

Selected by LEE BENNETT HOPKINS

Illustrated by KAREN BAUMANN

Harcourt Brace Jovanovich, Publishers

San Diego   New York   London

HBJ

*Permission acknowledgments appear on page 76,
which constitutes a continuation of the copyright page.*

*Library of Congress Cataloging-in-Publication Data
Ring out, wild bells: poems about holidays and seasons/selected by
Lee Bennett Hopkins; illustrated by Karen Baumann.
p.   cm.
Summary: A collection of poems about holidays and seasons,
organized chronologically from New Year to Christmas.
ISBN 0-15-267100-5
1. Holidays—Juvenile poetry. 2. Seasons—Juvenile poetry.
3. Children's poetry. [1. Holidays—Poetry. 2. Seasons—Poetry.
3. Poetry—Collections.] I. Hopkins, Lee Bennett. II. Baumann,
Karen, ill.
PN6110.H4R5   1992
821.008'033—dc20   89-20061*

BCDEF

*The illustrations in this book were done in Winsor & Newton
gouache on Strathmore 3-ply Bristol paper.
The display type was set in Latin Elongated.
The text type was set in Zapf International Light.
Composition by Thompson Type, San Diego, California
Color separations were made by Bright Arts, Ltd., Singapore.
Printed by The Eusey Press, Leominster, Massachusetts
Bound by Book Press, Inc., Brattleboro, Vermont
Production supervision by Warren Wallerstein and Fran Wager
Designed by Joy Chu*

Contents

Introduction   8

Introduction

Ring out, wild bells! — for the spinning of the seasons, for the holidays and rituals that mark the movement of each year.

Ring out for poetry, a remarkable genre that sharpens our senses, enhances the world, and helps us celebrate.

How much we enjoy the traditions that welcome each new season! Hundreds of years of culture, custom, wit, wisdom, folklore — and fun — are concentrated in these celebrations. They hold a special place in our hearts and present myriad opportunities to spark imaginations with rare images that only poetry can provide.

Only in poetry can a child's awareness of self and the exterior world be heightened so dramatically. Who but a poet would picture trees as "holding earth and sky together"? Who but a poet would remind us to be thankful for our noses on Thanksgiving day? Who but a poet would imagine Hawk spreading his wings to shelter the Christ child in the manger?

For me, a day without poetry is just another day on the calendar. And a holiday without poetry lacks some of the celebratory energy that links family and friends, children and grown-ups, past and future. Poetry carries the essence of these special days.

Because I believe that poetry is important, it was a particular pleasure to collect in one volume poems that vibrantly relate the changing of the seasons and the holidays. As a child I waited eagerly for these moments of the year, and as a classroom teacher I ushered in every season and each celebration with poetry.

In *Ring Out, Wild Bells* readers will discover poems — for occasions like Groundhog Day, April Fool's Day, Mother's Day, and Father's Day as well as for the ceremonial holidays such as Christmas and Hanukkah — that will bring the extra beauty, understanding, and joy to the day that only poetry can provide.

When is it time for poetry? It is always time for poetry. At the beginning of a school day, or tucked into a recess or lunch hour, in story time at the library, in homes at breakfast or bedtime. Holidays are certainly poetry days. But, ideally, every day should be a poetry day — for everyone.

Happy seasons, happy holidays, and happy poetry-ing to each and every one of you!

LEE BENNETT HOPKINS
Scarborough, New York
1992

from IN MEMORIAM

Ring out, wild bells, to the wild sky,
    The flying cloud, the frosty light:
    The year is dying in the night;
Ring out, wild bells, and let him die.

Ring out the old, ring in the new,
    Ring, happy bells, across the snow:
    The year is going, let him go;
Ring out the false, ring in the true.

Alfred, Lord Tennyson

NEW YEAR'S DAY

Last night, while we were fast asleep,
    The old year went away.
It can't come back again because
    A new one's come to stay.

Rachel Field

PROMISES

On New Year's Eve the snow came down
And covered every inch of town.
The next day winter sheets of white
Invited us to come and write
Our resolutions in the snow
So everyone in town would know
Of all the things we planned to do
To make the year completely new.

I dressed up warmly, then went out.
In single tracks I walked about,
Then found a spot ringed round with weeds
That seemed just perfect for my needs.
I took a breath and then jumped back
To keep a distance from my track,
And lay me down, my cheeks aglow,
To make an angel in the snow.

Jane Yolen

WELCOME TO THE NEW YEAR

Hey, my lad, ho, my lad!
  Here's a New Broom.
Heaven's your housetop
  And Earth is your room.

Tuck up your shirtsleeves,
  There's plenty to do—
Look at the muddle
  That's waiting for you!

Dust in the corners
  And dirt on the floor,
Cobwebs still clinging
  To window and door.

Hey, my lad! ho, my lad!
  Nimble and keen—
Here's your New Broom, my lad!
  See you sweep clean.

Eleanor Farjeon

MARTIN LUTHER KING DAY

The dream
of Martin Luther King
will happen
in some far-off Spring

when winter ice
and snow are gone.
One day, the dreamer
in gray dawn

will waken
to a blinding light
where hawk and dove
in silent flight

brush wings together
on a street
still thundering
with ghostly feet.

And soul will dance
and soul will sing
and march with
Martin Luther King.

Myra Cohn Livingston

GROUND HOG DAY

Ground Hog sleeps
All winter
Snug in his fur,
Dreams
Green dreams of
Grassy shoots,
Of nicely newly nibbly
Roots—
Ah, he starts to
Stir.
With drowsy
Stare
Looks from his burrow
Out on fields of
Snow.
What's there?
Oh no.
His shadow. Oh,
How sad!
Six more
Wintry
Weeks
To go.

Lilian Moore

VALENTINE FOR EARTH

Oh, it will be fine
To rocket through space
And see the reverse
Of the moon's dark face,

To travel to Saturn
Or Venus or Mars,
Or maybe discover
Some uncharted stars.

But do they have anything
Better than we?
Do you think, for instance,
They have a blue sea

For sailing and swimming?
Do the planets have hills
With raspberry thickets
Where a song sparrow fills

The summer with music?
And do they have snow
To silver the roads
Where the school buses go?

Oh, I'm all for rockets
And worlds cold or hot,
But I'm wild in love
With the planet we've got!

Frances Frost

THE BEST VALENTINE

Some valentines are paper,
Shaped like hearts of pink and gold.
Some valentines are flowers
In a soft green tissue fold.
Some valentines are candy,
But the one I got instead
Was a furry little puppy
With a collar that was red.

Margaret Hillert

SPEEDING VALENTINE

I made a racing valentine
with motor, wheels, and horn.
I drove it round and round the park
one February morn.
You jumped inside and rode with me,
co-pilot from the start,
as if you had been born to race
inside my zooming heart.

Sandra Liatsos

LINCOLN MONUMENT: WASHINGTON

Let's go see Old Abe
Sitting in the marble and the moonlight,
Sitting lonely in the marble and the moonlight,
Quiet for ten thousand centuries, old Abe.
Quiet for a million, million years.

Quiet—

And yet a voice forever
Against the
Timeless walls
Of time—
Old Abe.

Langston Hughes

GEORGE WASHINGTON'S BIRTHDAY: WONDERING

I wonder what I would have said
if my dad asked me,
"Son, do you know who cut down
my pretty cherry tree?"
I think I might have closed my eyes
and thought a little bit
about the herds of elephants
I'd seen attacking it.
I would have heard the rat-a-tat
of woodpeckers, at least,
or the raging roar of a charging boar
or some such other beast!
Perhaps a hippopotamus
with nothing else to do
had wandered through our garden
and stopped to take a chew.
We all know George said,
"Father, I cannot tell a lie."
Yet I can't help but wonder . . .
Did he *really* try?

Bobbi Katz

FIRST BIRTHDAY

Baby had a birthday party;
It wasn't lots of fun.
You don't know how to celebrate
When you are only One.

We sang the "Happy Birthday" song;
We clapped and made a fuss,
But Baby just ate Cheerios
Ignoring all of us.

Daddy brought the picture film—
(A hundred-year supply),
But Baby squirmed and tried to hide;
The FLASHES made him cry.

Mother opened all the gifts
That she had neatly wrapped,
While I enjoyed the birthday cake,
And Baby soundly napped.

Yes—someone had a party;
And "someone" had the fun,
But—that SOMEONE was *not* Baby,
When he was only One.

Barbara M. Hales

THE BIRTHDAY CHILD

Everything's been different
　All the day long,
Lovely things have happened,
　Nothing has gone wrong.

Nobody has scolded me,
　Everyone has smiled.
Isn't it delicious
　To be a birthday child?

Rose Fyleman

WEARING OF THE GREEN

It ought to come in April,
or, better yet in May
when everything is green as green—
I mean St. Patrick's Day.

With still a week of winter
this wearing of the green
seems rather out of season—
it's rushing things, I mean.

But maybe March is better
when all is done and said:
St. Patrick brings a promise,
a four-leaf-clover promise,
a green-all-over promise
of springtime just ahead!

Aileen Fisher

IF YOU BELIEVE ME

Lenny, sailing down the river,
Ate tons and tons of fresh-ground liver.

Peter, flying in the sky,
Ate gobs and gobs of pigsty pie.

Heather, sitting up in bed,
Ate chunks and chunks of codfish head.

Mickey, riding a caboose,
Ate slabs and slabs of uncooked moose.

Foods *so* tasty
Made them drool—

(If you believe me—
You're an

APRIL FOOL!)

Lee Bennett Hopkins

from TWO TRAMPS IN MUD TIME

The sun was warm but the wind was chill.
You know how it is with an April day
When the sun is out and the wind is still,
You're one month on in the middle of May.
But if you so much as dare to speak,
A cloud comes over the sunlit arch,
A wind comes off a frozen peak,
And you're two months back in the middle of March.

Robert Frost

WAKE UP

"Wake up," called the Sun to the trees,
"Wake up to the bright world about you,
Wake up baby buds from your long winter's sleep
For I can't start a new spring without you."

"Come back," called the Sun to the birds,
"Come back to your old homes and stay,
Come back, my friends, from your southern retreats
For I'm starting a new spring today."

"Come running," called the Sun at my door,
"Come running through meadows so new,
Come running and skipping and kicking your heels
For I'm getting spring ready for you."

Beverly McLoughland

SPRING

I'm shouting
I'm singing
I'm swinging through trees
I'm winging sky-high
With the buzzing black bees.
I'm the sun
I'm the moon
I'm the dew on the rose.
I'm a rabbit
Whose habit
Is twitching his nose.
I'm lively
I'm lovely
I'm kicking my heels.
I'm crying "Come dance"
To the freshwater eels.
I'm racing through meadows
Without any coat
I'm a gamboling lamb
I'm a light leaping goat
I'm a bud
I'm a bloom
I'm a dove on the wing.
I'm running on rooftops
And welcoming spring!

Karla Kuskin

ARBOR DAY: LET'S PLANT A TREE

It's time to plant a tree, a tree.
What shall it be? What shall it be?

Let's plant a pine—we can't go wrong:
a pine is green the whole year long.

Let's plant a maple—more than one,
to shade us from the summer sun.

Let's plant a cherry—you know why:
there's nothing like a cherry pie!

Let's plant an elm, the tree of grace,
where robins find a nesting place.

Let's plant an apple—not too small,
with flowers in spring and fruit in fall.

Let's plant a fir—so it can be
a lighted outdoor Christmas tree.

Let's plant a birch, an oak, a beech,
there's something extra-nice in each . . .
in winter, summer, spring or fall.
Let's plant a . . .

                 why not plant them ALL?

Aileen Fisher

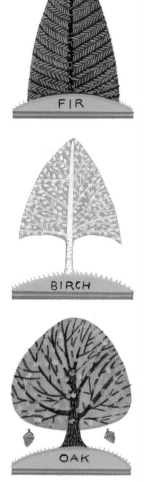

GRANDPA'S TREES

My grandpa built a farmhouse
Half a century ago.
On Arbor Day he planted trees
In one long tidy row.

He says they looked like beanpoles,
So leafless, frail and small.
He tended them those early years
Though they gave no shade at all.

Today I counted forty trees
Tall-grown, and sturdy-stout.
Their branches hug each other
As the wind blows them about.

They've sheltered Grandpa's farmhouse
In every sort of weather.
To me, they're friendly giants
Holding earth and sky together.

Barbara M. Hales

EASTER MORNING

We went out on an Easter morning
Under the trees and the wide blue sky,
Up to the hills where the buds were
   swelling—
Mother, Father, Puck and I.

And I had hopes that we'd see a rabbit,
A brown little one with a cotton tail,
So we looked in the woods and under the
   bushes,
And followed what seemed like a rabbit
   trail.

We peeked and poked. But there wasn't a
   rabbit
Wherever we'd look or wherever we'd go—
And then I remembered, and said,
   "NO WONDER,
Easter's their busiest day, you know!"

Aileen Fisher

AT EASTER TIME

The little flowers came through the ground,
  At Easter time, at Easter time:
They raised their heads and looked around,
  At happy Easter time.
And every pretty bud did say,
  "Good people, bless this holy day,
For Christ is risen, the angels say
  At happy Easter time!"

The pure white lily raised its cup
  At Easter time, at Easter time:
The crocus to the sky looked up
  At happy Easter time.
"We'll hear the song of Heaven!" they say,
  "Its glory shines on us today.
Oh! may it shine on us alway
  At holy Easter time!"

'Twas long and long and long ago,
  That Easter time, that Easter time:
But still the pure white lilies blow
  At happy Easter time.
And still each little flower doth say
  "Good Christians, bless this holy day,
For Christ is risen, the angels say
  At blessed Easter time!"

Laura E. Richards

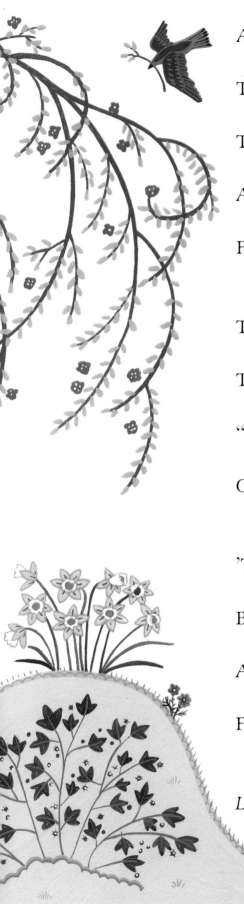

BACK YARD: BEFORE THE EGG HUNT

Lilacs, dressed for Easter,
Stand silently beside
The basement stair—purpling there;
What do they have to hide?

Willow branches touch the ground—
An early morning weep;
Yellow, green and in between—
What secrets do they keep?

By the fence tall grasses grown,
Morning glories, too.
Blues and reds, nodding their heads—
What do they keep from view?

Soon, I'll search beside the fence,
The willow and the stair;
I'll look hard throughout the yard—
I'll find what's hiding there.

Fran Haraway

EASTER

Purples,
      pinks,
           yellows,
               greens —

The prettiest hues ever seen.

Like carousel colors
they
leap
and
play;

Easter
is
a
RAINBOW

    day!

Lee Bennett Hopkins

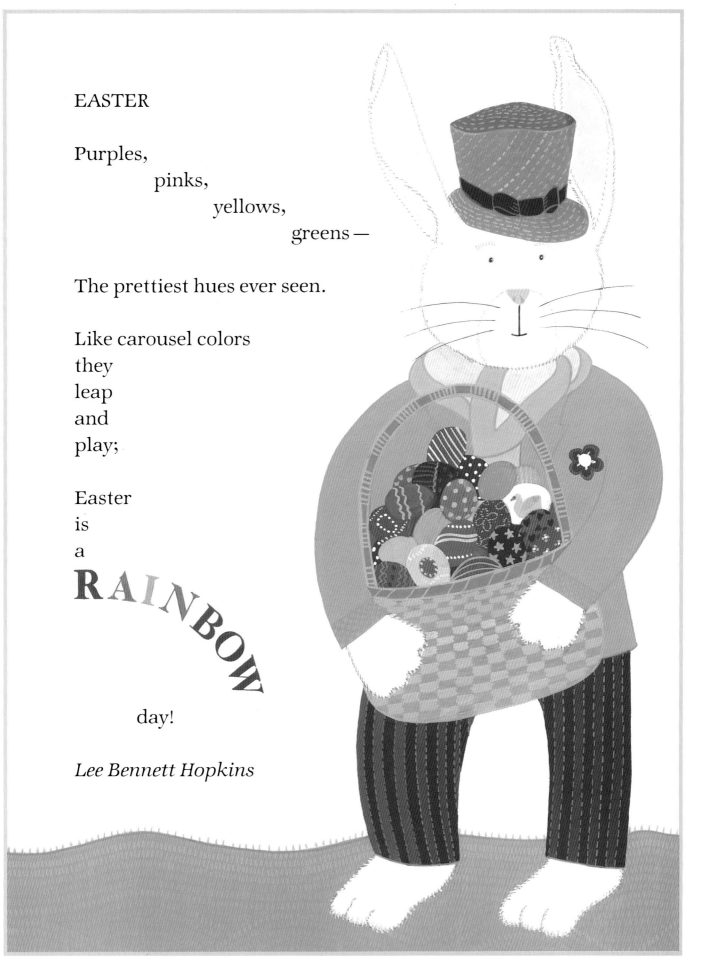

MAY DAY

On May Day
I was Maypole Queen.
I wore
a long
white
gown.
It turned
all brown
and muddy
from the rain
left
on the ground.

My golden wand
got broken
when we danced
the ribbons
round,
but the clover
and the daisies
are still
twining
in my
crown.

Myra Cohn Livingston

THERE IS BUT ONE MAY IN THE YEAR

There is but one May in the year,
   And sometimes May is wet and cold;
There is but one May in the year
   Before the year grows old.

Yet though it be the chilliest May,
   With least of sun and most of showers,
Its wind and dew, its night and day,
   Bring up the flowers.

Christina G. Rossetti

MOTHER TO SON

Well, son, I'll tell you:
Life for me ain't been no crystal stair.
It's had tacks in it,
And splinters,
And boards torn up,
And places with no carpet on the floor—
Bare.
But all the time
I'se been a-climbin' on,
And reachin' landin's,
And turnin' corners,
And sometimes goin' in the dark
Where there ain't been no light.
So, boy, don't you turn back.
Don't you set down on the steps
'Cause you finds it kinder hard.
Don't you fall now—
For I'se still goin', honey,
I'se still climbin',
And life for me ain't been no crystal stair.

Langston Hughes

NIGHT AND MORNING

The morning sits outside afraid
Until my mother draws the shade;

Then it bursts in like a ball,
Splashing sun all up the wall.

And the evening is not night
Until she's tucked me in just right
And kissed me and turned out the light.

Oh, if my mother went away
Who would start the night and day?

Dorothy Aldis

from THE PEOPLE, YES

"I love you,"
said a great mother.
"I love you for what you are
knowing so well what you are.
And I love you more yet, child,
deeper yet than ever, child,
for what you are going to be,
knowing so well you are going far,
knowing your great works are ahead,
ahead and beyond,
yonder and far over yet."

Carl Sandburg

MEMORIAL DAY

Daddy keeps the war in a shoebox
  tied up tight
                with a long white string.

On Memorial Day
  we open the box
                lift the lid
                        and look inside.

Dog tags and pins and stars and stripes
all jumbled together like prizes in a gumball machine.

        Then Daddy puts my hands in his
        and tells me about the war

And I feel the meaning of Memorial Day

                in the warmth of Daddy's hands.

Constance Andrea Keremes

MEMORIAL DAY

All the white markers
cannot tell
the tale of soldiers
we knew well.
Their faces fade
from memory,
but not their deeds,
which kept us free.
So let us praise them
on this day,
and all the time we
praise them pray
the day will come when
all wars cease,
and we will live in
love and peace.

Marci Ridlon

OUR FLAG

How bright our flag
against the sky
atop its flagpole
straight and high!

How bright the red,
the white, the blue,
with what they stand for
shining through,

More meaningful
as years go by . . .
how bright, how bright,
the flag we fly.

Aileen Fisher

FOR FATHER'S DAY

I found a seashell
for my dad,
just right for Father's Day.
I polished it
until it shone.
I hid it deep away.

When I gave it
to my dad
he held it to his ear
and told me I
had given him
the whole, wide sea to hear.

Sandra Liatsos

PAPA IS A BEAR

Papa is a morning bear —
Showers, pats his grizzly hair,
Throws his clothes on, scares the cat,
Shuffles down to breakfast. That
Closet is his hiding place,
BOO!, hugs Mama, rubs my face
With his whiskers, eats his grits,
Growls again before he sits
In his den to read the news,
Winks at me, unties his shoes;
Papa's ready for a snooze.

J. Patrick Lewis

TO JULY

Here's to July.
Here's to July.
For the bird,
And the bee,
And the butterfly;
For the flowers
That blossom
For feasting the eye;

For skates, balls,
And jump ropes,
For swings that go high;
For rocketry
Fireworks that
Blaze in the sky,
Oh, here's to July.

Anonymous

FOURTH OF JULY PARADE

Hear the blare of bugles,
Hear the beat of drums,
Hear the sound of marching feet.
Down the street there comes,
   Playing, marching,
   Marching, playing,
   In the sun and shade,
   All the music,
   All the color
   Of the Fourth's parade.

See the buglers blowing,
See the drummers pound,
See the feet go up and down
To the music's sound.
   Playing, marching,
   Marching, playing,
   In the shade and sun,
   All the color,
   All the music,
   Says the Fourth's begun.

Anonymous

FOURTH OF JULY NIGHT

The little boat at anchor
in black water sat murmuring
to the tall black sky.

. . .

A white sky bomb fizzed on a black line.
A rocket hissed its red signature into the west.
Now a shower of Chinese fire alphabets,
a cry of flower pots broken in flames,
a long curve to a purple spray,
three violet balloons —
    Drips of seaweed tangled in gold,
    shimmering symbols of mixed numbers,
    tremulous arrangements of cream gold folds
    of a bride's wedding gown —

. . .

A few sky bombs spoke their pieces,
then velvet dark.

The little boat at anchor
in black water sat murmuring
to the tall black sky.

Carl Sandburg

SUNFLAKES

If sunlight fell like snowflakes,
gleaming yellow and so bright,
we could build a sunman,
we could have a sunball fight,
we could watch the sunflakes
drifting in the sky.
We could go sleighing
in the middle of July
through sundrifts and sunbanks,
we could ride a sunmobile,
and we could touch sunflakes —
I wonder how they'd feel.

Frank Asch

AUGUST

The sprinkler twirls.
  The summer wanes.
The pavement wears
  Popsicle stains.

The playground grass
  Is worn to dust.
The weary swings
  Creak, creak with rust.

The trees are bored
  With being green.
Some people leave
  The local scene

And go to seaside
  Bungalows
And take off nearly
  All their clothes.

John Updike

WHAT SHALL I PACK IN THE BOX MARKED "SUMMER"?

A handful of wind that I caught with a kite
A firefly's flame in the dark of the night
The green grass of June that I tasted with toes
The flowers I knew from the tip of my nose
The clink of the ice cubes in pink lemonade
The Fourth of July Independence parade!
The sizzle of hot dogs, the fizzle of Coke
Some pickles and mustard and barbecue smoke
The print of my fist in the palm of my mitt.
As I watched for the batter to strike out or hit
The splash of the water, the top-to-toe cool
Of a stretch-and-kick trip through a blue swimming pool
The tangle of night songs that slipped through my screen
Of crickets and insects too small to be seen
The seed pods that formed on the flowers to say
That summer was packing her treasures away.

Bobbi Katz

LABOR DAY

First Monday in September
that's when we remember
to honor workers who toil long.
Their efforts make our country strong.
We give a gift they all like best;
We give them all a day of rest!

Marci Ridlon

NOW

Close the barbecue.
Close the sun.
Close the home-run games we won.

Close the picnic.
Close the pool.

Close the summer.

Open school.

Prince Redcloud

TASTE OF PURPLE

Grapes hang purple
In their bunches,
Ready for
September lunches.
Gather them, no
Minutes wasting.
Purple is
Delicious tasting.

Leland B. Jacobs

NOCTURN CABBAGE

Cabbages catch at the moon.
It is late summer, no rain, the pack of the soil
    cracks open, it is a hard summer.

In the night the cabbages catch at the moon, the
    leaves drip silver, the rows of cabbages are
    series of little silver waterfalls in the moon.

Carl Sandburg

ROSH HASHANAH

Rosh Hashanah. The shofar blows.
The new year comes. The old year goes.
Rosh Hashanah. The new year starts
With a fine feeling in our hearts,
One we can keep the whole year through
In the things we say and the things we do.

Listen, listen. The shofar blows
As the new year comes and the old one goes.

Margaret Hillert

12 OCTOBER

From where I stand now
   the world is flat,
   flat out flat,
   no end to that.

   Where my eyes go the land moves out.

   How is it then
   five hundred years ago (about)
   Columbus found
   that far beyond the flat on flat
   the world was round?

Myra Cohn Livingston

AUTUMN WOODS

I like the woods
  In autumn
When dry leaves hide the ground,
When the trees are bare
And the wind sweeps by
With a lonesome rushing sound.

I can rustle the leaves
  In autumn
And I can make a bed
In the thick dry leaves
That have fallen
From the bare trees
Overhead.

James S. Tippett

THEME IN YELLOW

I spot the hills
With yellow balls in autumn.
I light the prairie cornfields
Orange and tawny gold clusters
And I am called pumpkins.
On the last of October
When dusk is fallen
Children join hands
And circle round me
Singing ghost songs
And love to the harvest moon;
I am a jack-o'-lantern
With terrible teeth
And the children know
I am fooling.

Carl Sandburg

PUMPKINS

October sun for miles and miles and miles;
and we were passing piles and piles and piles
of pumpkins—pumpkin-like, so like each other
no pumpkin knew one pumpkin from his brother.
If they were carved and placed in aisles and aisles,
with piles and piles of smiles and smiles and smiles
for miles and miles and miles on some dark night,
and one could handle, candle them, and light
the whole creation with Jack Pumpkinheads,
they'd be no wiser. What a pumpkin dreads
is being so conspicuous with eyes
and nose and mouth. Much better off in pies,
say pumpkins. So for miles and miles and miles,
with piles of pumpkins—aisles and aisles of piles—
just putting all their pumpkinheads together,
you couldn't tell what they were thinking: whether
they thought of Halloween, or where they grew
in yellow pumpkin fields. I'd say the view
was pleasing to those pumpkins at the top—
which were of course the best ones in the crop.
But since they had no eyes nowise to know,
they might as well have been down there below;
nor could they guess that mile on mile on mile
some boy was hoping he might see one smile.

David McCord

HALLOWEEN CONCERT

"It's cold," said the cricket,
"my fingers are numb.
I scarcely can fiddle,
I scarcely can strum.
And oh, I'm so sleepy,
now summer has gone."
He dropped his fiddle
to stifle a yawn.

"Don't," said the field mouse, "act so sober.
You can't stop *yet*, when it's still October."

"I've played," said the cricket,
"for weeks and weeks.
My fiddle needs fixing,
it's full of squeaks.
My fingers need resting."
He yawned. "Ho, hum . . .
I'm quite (yawn) ready . . .
for winter to come.
I've found the coziest . . .
              doziest . . .
              house . . ."

"You can't stop *now*," said his friend, the mouse.

"No?" yawned the cricket,
and closed his eyes.
"I've played so much
for a chap my size,
it's time (he yawned)
for my winter snooze:
I hear the creak
of November's shoes."

"You can't," said the mouse in a voice of sorrow,
"you *can't* stop fiddling until tomorrow.
Tune up your fiddle for one last
    scene . . .
have you forgotten it's Halloween?"

"What!" cried the cricket.
He yawned no more!
"You should have mentioned
the fact before.
Is everyone ready?
And where's the score?
What in the world
are we waiting for?"

(continued)

The cricket fiddled,
the field mouse squeaked,
the dry weeds twiddled,
the bare twigs tweaked,
the hoot owl hooted,
the cornstalks strummed,
the west winds tooted,
the fence wires hummed:

Oh, what a concert, all night long!
The fiddle was shrill, and the wind was strong:

"Halloween, Halloween,
crick,
crack,
creak.

Halloween, Halloween,
scritch,
scratch,
squeak."

Aileen Fisher

AUTUMN GHOST SOUNDS

When the moon
rides high,
up overhead—
and I am snug
and warm,
in bed—
in the autumn dark
the ghosts move 'round,
making their
mournful
moaning sound.

I listen to know
when the ghosts
go by.
I hear a wail,
and I hear a sigh.

But I can't quite tell
which I hear
the most—
the wind,
or the wail
of some passing ghost.

Anonymous

HALLOWEEN

Hooting
 Howling
  Hissing
   Witches;

Riding
 Rasping
  Ragged
   Switches;

Fluttering
 Frightening
  Fearsome
   Bats;

Arching
 Awesome
  Awful
   Cats;

Lone
 Lantern-
  Lighted
   Streets;

Tricks!
 Tasty
  Tempting
   Treats!

Phyllis J. Perry

SOMETHING TOLD THE WILD GEESE

Something told the wild geese
 It was time to go.
Though the fields lay golden
 Something whispered, "Snow."
Leaves were green and stirring,
 Berries, luster-glossed,
But beneath warm feathers
 Something cautioned, "Frost."
All the sagging orchards
 Steamed with amber spice,
But each wild breast stiffened
 At remembered ice.
Something told the wild geese
 It was time to fly—
Summer sun was on their wings,
 Winter in their cry.

Rachel Field

LITTLE LONG SLEEPER

Now in November,
Ladybug finds a cozy crack
in my windowsill.

See her remember
to set her dainty alarm clock
for early spring.

Sleep sound, Lady, until
you hear it ring.

Norma Farber

THANKSGIVING

Thank You
   for all my hands can hold—
      apples red
      and melons gold,
         yellow corn
            both ripe and sweet,
            peas and beans
               so good to eat!

Thank You
   for all my eyes can see—
      lovely sunlight,
      field and tree,
         white cloud-boats
            in sea-deep sky,
            soaring bird
               and butterfly.

Thank You
   for all my ears can hear—
      birds' songs echoing
      far and near,
         songs of little
            stream, big sea,
            cricket, bullfrog,
               duck and bee!

Ivy O. Eastwick

THANKSGIVING

The year has turned its circle,
The seasons come and go.
The harvest is all gathered in
And chilly north winds blow.

Orchards have shared their treasures,
The fields, their yellow grain,
So open wide the doorway—
Thanksgiving comes again!

Anonymous

FIRST THANKSGIVING

Venison for stew and roasting,
oysters in the ashes toasting,
geese done to a turn,
berries (dried) and wild grapes (seeded)
mixed with dough and gently kneaded—
what a feast to earn!

Indian corn in strange disguises,
ash cakes, hoe cakes (many sizes),
kernels roasted brown . . .
after months of frugal living
what a welcome first Thanksgiving
there in Plymouth town!

Aileen Fisher

A THANKSGIVING THOUGHT

The day I give thanks for having a nose
Is Thanksgiving Day, for do you suppose
That Thanksgiving dinner would taste as good
If you couldn't smell it? I don't think it would.
Could apple pies baking—turkey that's basting
Not be for smelling? Just be for tasting?
It's a cranberry-cinnamon-onion bouquet!
Be thankful for noses on Thanksgiving Day.

Bobbi Katz

A WINTER SONG

If I
were the
cold weather
and people
talked about me
the way they talk
about it,
I'd just
pack up
and leave town.

William J. Harris

WINTER MORNING

Winter is the king of showmen,
Turning tree stumps into snow men
And houses into birthday cakes
And spreading sugar over lakes.
Smooth and clean and frosty white,
The world looks good enough to bite.
That's the season to be young,
Catching snowflakes on your tongue.

Snow is snowy when it's snowing,
I'm sorry it's slushy when it's going.

Ogden Nash

JOE'S SNOW CLOTHES

For wandering walks
In the sparkling snow
No one is muffled
More warmly than Joe.
No one is mittened more,
Coated or hatted,
Booted or sweatered,
Both knitted and tatted,
Buttoned and zippered,
Tied, tucked and belted,
Padded and wadded
And quilted and felted,
Hooked in and hooded,
Tweeded and twilled.
Nothing of Joe's
From his top to his toes
But the tip of his nose
Could be touched
By the snows
Or the wind as it blows,
And grow rather rosy,
The way a nose grows
If it's frozen
Or possibly chilled.

Karla Kuskin

FAMILY HANUKKAH

Mother's in the kitchen frying
Potato pancakes, crisp and light,
Father hides the children's presents
To be opened every night.
Amy shines the brass menorah
Till it glitters like the sun,
David counts the tiny candles,
He will light them one by one.
Grandma bustles round the household,
Then Grandpa joins the Hanukkah fun,
He tells the Maccabean story,
A family Hanukkah has begun!

Eva Grant

COMPARISON

Chanukah—a time for celebration
Chanukah—the Feast of Dedication
Chanukah—eight candles shining bright
Re-create the miracle of light.

Christmas—time for great festivity
Christmas—celebrate Nativity
Christmas—one star radiating light
Symbol of the miracle that night.

Fran Haraway

IN THE WEEK WHEN CHRISTMAS COMES

This is the week when Christmas comes.

Let every pudding burst with plums,
And every tree bear dolls and drums,
In the week when Christmas comes.

Let every hall have boughs of green,
With berries glowing in between,
In the week when Christmas comes.

Let every doorstep have a song
Sounding the dark street along,
In the week when Christmas comes.

Let every steeple ring a bell
With a joyful tale to tell,
In the week when Christmas comes.

Let every night put forth a star
To show us where the heavens are,
In the week when Christmas comes.

Let every stable have a lamb
Sleeping warm beside its dam,
In the week when Christmas comes.

This is the week when Christmas comes.

Eleanor Farjeon

NORTH AND SOUTH

Christmas again,
holly and pine,
bells and berries,
things that shine.

Christmas again,
but far away
palm trees drip
with ocean spray!
Far away it's very sunny
but here it's cold and white . . .
            it's funny.

Charlotte Zolotow

THE TWENTY-FOURTH OF DECEMBER

The clock ticks slowly,
slowly
in the hall,
And slower and more slow
the long hours crawl;
It seems as though today
Will never pass away;
The clock ticks slowly

    s-l-o-w-l-y

in the hall.

Anonymous

from GO TELL IT ON THE MOUNTAIN

Go tell it on the mountain,
Over the hills and everywhere,
Go tell it on the mountain,
That Jesus Christ is born.

Anonymous

FROM HEAVEN HIGH I COME TO YOU

From Heaven high I come to you;
I bring you news both good and true.
Glad tidings of great joy I bring;
To you is born this night a King.

To you is born this night a Child,
Of Virgin Mary meek and mild;
A Child so blessed, and full of love,
Sent for your joy from Heaven above.

Martin Luther

CAROL OF THE BROWN KING

Of the three Wise Men
Who came to the King,
One was a brown man,
So they sing.

Of the three Wise Men
Who followed the Star,
One was a brown king
From afar.

They brought fine gifts
Of spices and gold
In jeweled boxes
Of beauty untold.

Unto His humble
Manger they came
And bowed their heads
In Jesus' name.

Three Wise Men,
One dark like me —
Part of His
Nativity.

Langston Hughes

WHEN IT SNOWED THAT NIGHT UPON A STABLE

When it snowed that night upon a stable,
and the roof leaked water in the hay—

Hawk spread his wings across the manger,
Camel lap-lapped a puddle dry,
Lamb rolled around in her fleece
to sponge up the drops, dripping,
Lizard clung fast to a ceiling-hole,
Heron plugged a gap with his beak,
Woodpecker pegged a tiny chink
with a right-sized splinter,
Giraffe held his head against a crack,
Bat flung his web across another,
Sloth pressed his palm against a third—

and the three Grand Kings
raised a parasol over the family.

Norma Farber

TIME FOR CHRISTMAS

What says it's time for Christmas?
    Is it the merry bells?
Or is it when the kitchen
    is sweet with spicy smells?

Or do we know when packages
    are hiding in the hall?
Or when the tree, all tinseled,
    stands rainbow-bright and tall?

Is it caroling . . . or candy canes,
    or teddy bears, or drums . . .

Is it dolls, or toys, or puddings,
    that tell when Christmas comes?

What says *best* "It's Christmas!"
    Is it all these things?
Or is it when we feel the Love
    that Christmas always brings?

Joan Walsh Anglund

LITTLE TREE

little tree
little silent Christmas tree
you are so little
you are more like a flower

who found you in the green forest
and were you very sorry to come away?
see   i will comfort you
because you smell so sweetly

i will kiss your cool bark
and hug you safe and tight
just as your mother would,
only don't be afraid

look   the spangles
that sleep all the year in a dark box
dreaming of being taken out and allowed to shine,
the balls the chains red and gold the fluffy threads,

put up your little arms
and i'll give them all to you to hold
every finger shall have its ring
and there won't be a single place dark or unhappy

then when you're quite dressed
you'll stand in the window for everyone to see
and how they'll stare!
oh but you'll be very proud

and my little sister and i will take hands
and looking up at our beautiful tree
we'll dance and sing
"Noel Noel"

e. e. cummings

KALEIDOSCOPE

Chock-full boxes, packages—
squeeze 'em, feel sharp angles!
From candycaned
evergreen
a tinfoil
rainfall

dangles.

Cold-tongued bells are tolling,
tolling, *Hark, the herald*
angels sing
Christ the King!
Earth's
rebirth

is caroled.

Sheep and ox guard manger
Magi offer gifts.
Down through white
silent night
slow
snow

sifts.

X. J. Kennedy

SNOW

Softly
whitely
down
the snow
mounds
and sifts
in dunes
in drifts
coldly
sowing
fields
of clover
covering
December
over.

Felice Holman

END OF A YEAR

spring to summer,
summer to fall,
goodbye, oh year,
goodbye;
fall to winter,
winter to spring,
(one more time for the birds to sing,
one more day for the earth to bloom,
one time yet for the burning sun,
one more moment and then it's done),
goodbye, oh year,
goodbye.

Patricia Hubbell

Permission Acknowledgments

Every effort has been made to trace the ownership of all copyrighted material and to secure the necessary permission to reprint these selections. In the event of any question arising as to the use of any material, the editor and the publisher, while expressing regret for any inadvertent error, will be happy to make the necessary correction in future printings. Thanks are due to the following for permission to reprint the copyrighted materials listed below:

Abingdon Press for "Thanksgiving" from *Cherry Stones! Garden Swings!* by Ivy O. Eastwick. Copyright renewed © 1990 by Hooper and Wollen, executors for estate of Ivy O. Eastwick. Used by permission of Abingdon Press.

Curtis Brown, Ltd. for "Easter" by Lee Bennett Hopkins, copyright © 1979 by Lee Bennett Hopkins; "If You Believe Me" by Lee Bennett Hopkins, copyright © 1992 by Lee Bennett Hopkins; "Promises" by Jane Yolen, copyright © 1986 by Jane Yolen. All reprinted by permission of Curtis Brown, Ltd.

Doubleday, Inc. for "New Year's Day" from *A Little Book of Days* by Rachel Field. Copyright 1927 by Doubleday, a division of Bantam, Doubleday, Dell Publishing Group, Inc. Used by permission of the publisher.

Thomas Farber for "Little Long Sleeper" and "When It Snowed That Night upon a Stable" by Norma Farber. Copyright Thomas Farber.

Aileen Fisher for "Easter Morning" from *That's Why* (Nelson, NY, 1946), copyright renewed; "Halloween Concert" first published in *Story Parade*, 1951. All rights controlled by Aileen Fisher.

Frances Frost's "Valentine for Earth" from *The Little Naturalist* (McGraw-Hill). Copyright © 1959 by Frances Frost.

Barbara M. Hales for "First Birthday" and "Grandpa's Trees." Used by permission of the author, who controls all rights.

Fran Haraway for "Back Yard: Before the Egg Hunt" and "Comparison." Used by permission of the author, who controls all rights.

Harcourt Brace Jovanovich, Inc. for "Theme in Yellow" from *Chicago Poems* by Carl Sandburg, copyright 1916 by Holt, Rinehart & Winston, Inc., copyright renewed 1944 by Carl Sandburg; excerpt from *The People, Yes* by Carl Sandburg, copyright 1936 by Harcourt Brace Jovanovich, Inc. and renewed 1964 by Carl Sandburg; "Nocturn Cabbage" from *Good Morning, America*, copyright 1928 and renewed 1956 by Carl Sandburg; "Fourth of July Night" from *Wind Song* by Carl Sandburg, copyright © 1960 by Carl Sandburg, renewed 1988 by Margaret Sandburg, Janet Sandburg, and Helga Sandburg Crile; "North and South" from *Everything Glistens and Everything Sings* by Charlotte Zolotow, copyright © 1987 by Charlotte Zolotow. All reprinted by permission of Harcourt Brace Jovanovich, Inc.

HarperCollins, Inc. for "Our Flag" and "First Thanksgiving" from *Skip Around the Year* by Aileen Fisher (Crowell), copyright © 1967 by Aileen Fisher; "Joe's Snow Clothes" and "Spring" from *Dogs & Dragons, Trees & Dreams* by Karla Kuskin, copyright © 1980 by Karla Kuskin; "In the Week When Christmas Comes" and "Welcome to the New Year" from *Poems for Children* by Eleanor Farjeon (Lippincott), copyright 1927, 1955 by Eleanor Farjeon, originally appeared in *Come Christmas* by Eleanor Farjeon; "Autumn Woods" from *Crickety-Cricket!* by James S. Tippett, copyright 1933 by Harper & Row, Publishers, Inc., renewed 1961 by Martha S. Tippett, originally appeared in *A World to Know*. All selections reprinted by permission of Harper & Row, Publishers, Inc.

Index of Authors

Index of Titles

Index of
First Lines